LIVING IN A RED STATE BLUES

M. Scott Douglass

Paycock Press
Arlington, Virginia

Cover art and book design: M. Scott Douglass

Acknowledgments:

Grateful appreciation to these publications and their editors for publishing poems included in this book, sometimes in different versions:

> *Gargoyle* (online): "Living in a Red State Blues, Pt 1,"
> "Clothing for Sale," "Erasing a Color from Literature,"
>   "Harmony"
> *North American Review*: "Living in a Red State Blues, Part 2"
> *Twelve Mile Review*: "It Is What It Is," "Legacy"
>
> Anthology
>   *Crossing the Rift: North Carolina Poets on 9/11 and its*
>   *Aftermath* (Press 53, 2021): "Twenty Years Later"

Library of Congress Control Number: 2022933080

ISBN-10: 0-931181-78-X
ISBN-13: 978-0-931181-78-8

Paycock Press
3819 North 13th Street
Arlington, VA 22201
gargoylepaycock.wordpress.com

for Jill (as always)

&

my father, Bill Douglass, Jr. (Moo)

&

Red America
whose antics made these poems
so easy to write

Contents

Foreword

It was late 2018. Could have been November or December—I don't remember, but I'm sure I could look it up in my medical bills. I had just bought a new Harley Davidson followed by knee replacement surgery—the latter ensuring that it would be a while before I could properly introduce myself to the former, but there were other surgical repercussions as well. For one thing, I had more time for circumspection. For another, I got a free "pass" from attending the annual neighborhood Christmas party. And that's where this collection of poems began to take shape.

About a year or so later, I thought I had something cohesive developing that I could put into a book format. Being a publisher myself, I went about doing the same work I would advise my poetry authors to do: *get the individual pieces published in literary magazines.*

I was encouraged by early responses, poems that were accepted in 2020 and published later that year and into 2021. But after that early wave, nothing. This was the height of the pandemic, nearing the time of the 2020 election and afterward into 2021.

Not all literary magazines were operating at full speed at this time. Nonetheless, I was discouraged by the lack of acceptnces. After a while, I set the collection aside. Sometimes looking at things through a longer lens allows you to see them more clearly.

I kept writing and new pieces kept fitting into the same overall theme, but I realized from the work I was seeing submitted to my own magazine, that it may not have been the work itself or the lack of personnel. It may have been the subject. The people on the reading end may have been burned out by it. Perhaps they were eager to move on from this period in our history or tired of hearing angry voices—no matter what they were angry about.

I've heard this referred to as being *canceled.* In reference to this collection, I prefer to think of it as *exhaustion.* Either way, by the time I returned from my motorcycle trip across

America during June/July 2021, I decided that this collection might never get published. It had no readership and thereby no market.

But there were some wins in 2021. Joseph Bathanti invited me to submit a poem to an anthology he was editing and that stirred me to write a new piece that fit both the anthology subject and the theme of my collection. That was followed by Robert Kendrick of *Twenty Mile Review* inviting me to send some work. I like crashing a party through bay windows as much as the next guy, but getting *invited* is a whole different thrill. This was a nice torch in a recently dark cave of rejection.

On January 17, 2022, I got an email from Richard Peabody that read:

"I want to run

Living in a Red State Blues, Pt 1
Clothing for Sale
Erasing a Color from Literature
Harmony

in Online Garg #1.

To queue this up, I didn't even know there was an *Online Gargoyle* in the planning let alone about to be launched. I had sent Richard an early version of this collection in April 2021. I asked if he thought it was worth pursuing further and whether it was something he would be interested in publishing on his Paycock Press label, the same one on which my previous book, *Just Passing Through* had been published in 2017.

Richard and I go back a long way together—so there is/ was no pressure to take anything. I was mostly looking for feedback. A publishing home was secondary. Within a week or so—and that's fast for Richard as those of you who have worked with him can attest—he shot back the inimitable, depth-defying answer of, "Sure."

Sure what? *Sure,* I should pursue it? *Sure* you would publish it? I decided, at the time, to assume both, not really certain whether it was the case or not. Call me an optimist.

His January 2022 message got me fired up again. I hadn't looked at this collection since the previous August. With 2022 now upon us, primaries and mid-terms upcoming, and the topic being what it was, if *Living in a Red State Blues* was to get published, it had to be this year.

I went back and re-read it. Re-reading equals rewriting. And then there were a few gaps that needed to be filled to make it more cohesive—so I wrote and added a few poems. After that, it was pestering a cadre of editors and friends and friendly editors to get some feedback followed by more editing.

Which brings us to where we are now.

I've done my part. My editors have added their two cents. It's up to you, readers. You can decide for yourselves whether I should have moved on to other things or placed it out there for reader scrutiny. I will happily live with the decision no matter what it may be. At least I will have said my piece and can be at peace with what I said.

M. Scott Douglass

And the people bowed and prayed
To the neon god they made

~ Simon & Garfunkel
from "Sound of Silence"

I

Erasing a Color (from Literature)

"Better dead than red." ~The Nation, *July 9, 1930*

Can we start with a version
where the wheelbarrow is green
or purple or orange?

    I'm not paranoid, I'm
    not paranoid, I'm not...

... *a chicken.* I'm a bluebird
scavenging seeds, scraps
spilled from a feeder above,

wary of cats that lurk nearby,
hidden among the chaos
of apathetic undergrowth.

Living in a Red State Blues, Part 1

The couple across the street props
an old pallet dressed in red, white,
and blue like a flag in their front yard
beside another hand-painted sign
that reads, "Put God back in America."

At Christmas, they host the neighborhood
dinner, make everyone pray before we eat.
A retired Marine, he lays his gun collection
across the bed where we store our coats.

In their not-so-private hours, we know
they curse Obama and *witch hunts* and chant
things like *lock her up* and *build a wall*. They go
to church each Sunday and Wednesday,
sing gospels with other faithful.

We decked our house with blue lights this year
and skipped the neighborhood dinner. If
the event ran true to form, some neighbors
were wheeled in, others hobbled behind
aluminum walkers.

All would have held hands in group prayer,
praised Donald Trump, discussed church events,
how wonderful the dry ham is, healthcare costs,
medications, vaccine and mask mandates.

My hands would have sweat through
the pretense and piousness.

They've fenced facts into a cage in
the back yard, feed it only when they can't
afford not to, invite neighbors over once a year to see
how well-behaved it is, how nicely they decorate
this world in which they've barricaded themselves.

I feel myself building a wall of my own,
one day at a time, one brick of truth mortared
to another. I'm already the neighborhood heathen.
Soon, they will cordon me off from the righteous,
censure me, protect the flock from anything
that might disturb the comfort of groupthink.

A Red-letter Kind of Day

Raise a red flag.
The redcoats are coming.
Redlegs are plotting another raid.
We're operating in the red and nobody cares.
Paint the town deceitful red, wave
a red hanky in the face of proud boy bull.
It's a red herring.
They were caught red-handed.
The Woody Woodpecker crew stuck
their heads up Mr. Potato Head's ass,
but it's all fake news, nothing new, you're
better off dead than red in the head, anyway.
Meanwhile the commies are coming
and going, Red China lands on
the red planet, the Cincinnati Reds
and Boston Red Sox swap logos,
Washington and Cleveland scrap
the bad imagery altogether.
Red Skelton was a red-headed stepchild
of Red Ryder until Red Barry put
a gun to his head. I hear
the Red-Hot Chili Peppers
tuning their instruments
for a tour of the red-light district.
There's a haughty redhead waiting
for them outside Red Rocks
or is it Red Lion, PA?
Anyway, they will all
surely tread the red carpet
as America sees itself
embroiled in red-faced lies,
a red snapper flip-flopping on
the deck of a slowly sinking ship.

And here I am, your average
red-blooded American boy
whose whole life is written in red ink
and all I want to do is cancel
my Red Hat Society membership,
avoid the red tape, catch a redeye home.

Cone of Uncertainty

Some people enter your life
like a hurricane, an angry
deluge of bitter bluster,
turn your home inside out,
its contents scattered, mangled,
blown up against your neighbors'
or flushed out to sea on
a twisting torrent of madness.
They stay too long, and when
they leave, they leave you
nothing, they leave you stranded
amid the clutter of a broken world
without so much as a wave goodbye.
As if a lover had dumped you
by tweet, spun the words out
across the globe for all to see.
In the end, you live with
the consolation that you
survived this oppressive storm,
that its maniacal term came
and went, a lonely blip
on history's radar, and despite
its most expansive efforts,
Alabama had still been spared.

Clothes for Sale

Mostly shirts, like new,
barely worn in several years
because I can't wear red anymore—
the color has been commandeered
by lurid ideology, corrupted
in ways that make me ashamed
to be seen wearing it in public.
Even certain shades of pink
and burgundy are now suspect—
though not abundant in this collection.
I would donate them all
to Goodwill, but I doubt anyone
who shops there would be more
comfortable in them than me,
and those who would shop
for items like these
need to pay a higher price.
I'd like to sell them as a group,
will accept best offer, but realize
the market for such things
is quickly shrinking.
I would turn them into rags,
but the color is now so stained,
I can't imagine anything
it could clean.

At the CPAC Revival

They rolled a golden calf
dressed in red, white,
and blue Bermuda shorts
and sandals into
the revival tent
to reunite the faithful
with their chosen one.
In his hand he held
a magic wand because
everyone knew no
miracle was pending
and magic was
the only thing
that could make
this fantasy come true.

Early Voting
October 15, 2020

We arrive as the glow of overnight
streetlights fades. A line at the door signaling
that we were not the only anxious voters
on this first day of *Early Voting*.

By the time the gate swings open, the line
has banked and stretched, social distancing
more than two football fields long. People
with walkers, canes, wheelchairs. People
wearing masks. People packing resolve like
a suitcase filled with a full day's necessities.

In the school yard, beside the lined-up voters,
a table of happy black women hand out flyers
for Democratic candidates. On the other side
of the line, Republicans stand with handouts,
butted up against a sign that reads:

> **No Campaigning**
> **Beyond This Point**

An elderly white man in a red MAGA hat
and no mask makes several passes, offers
a list of conservative judges.

There were only a few takers.

The doors open. We all move toward
the goal line. MAGA hat guy removes
his jacket, revealing a red t-shirt that proclaims:

> "I am one of the DEPLORABLES
> and Unredeemable"

I smile at his shirt, realizing that progress
had been made here today; an unnegotiated
silent debate resolved, delivering that ever-
elusive political unicorn of *common ground*.

A42N81

Dougie calls it *wind therapy*,
the remedy to a rough day,
a long winter, whatever ails you.
If you're lucky, you can jump
on a motorcycle, open it up, blow
all the bullshit the world dumps
on you to the side of the road.
I waited until late afternoon,
after a weekend sauna subsided,
to ride, then pushed it full throttle.
A cop stopped me on 218, walked up
and asked for the usual: *license and registration*.
As I dug them out of my wallet, he asked,
"Do you know how fast you were going?"
"Not really," I said, "I try to match
the speed of the vehicles around me."
He looked up and down the 2-lane highway,
said, "Sir, there were no vehicles around you."
"Well, therein lies the problem, I guess,"
slipped from my lips like a sneaky fart.
He snatched the ID from my hand,
gave me a blank, state trooper stare,
stood for a second, one hand slapping
the other with my papers, the pasture
behind me reflected in his glasses.
Then he handed my stuff back and said,
"Have a nice day, sir," and walked away,
tossing these words over his shoulder:
"And slow the hell down, will ya?"
"Absolutely," I said, as I cranked the engine
and rolled out into the wind's warm embrace,
wondering if the outcome would have
been the same, if I were a black man.

Breathless

Sometimes you find
         your voice
      by the side of a road
a road everyone
               walks
everyone drives
         you find it
      like a discarded
paper cup
         dancing
in the wind
         until flattened
      by a passing semi
dirty   aged   ragged
         but no less vibrant
than the rhythm
               of your own
aberrant heart

Confrontageous

In a word, my ex had said
it all: the instability of
his disposition, a shared
trait handed down from me
through my son, to
my grandson—
       only he's worse.
As if we—my son and I—
had refined and funneled
our combined rage
into a chromosomal
assault weapon able
to blast away any and all
anomalies, opposing
or blended familial factors;
a personality trait distilled
down to a solitary source
of frustration. Or maybe
she believes proximity
to a super-spreader
dispersed an infection
in search of a cure.
More than anything,
       with a single word
she exposed the keystone
to our legendary lack
of communication.

Red Walks into a Bar

It's not his usual bar, his
usual crowd. It could be any bar
in any bumpkin town any-
where in America.

      Everyone knows Red. Everyone
      knows his hat, his shirt, his swagger.

He always orders top shelf, waits
for the *oohs* and *ahs* to fade
before scoping the room to see
who's watching him.

Chicks dig Red, they like riding
in his red Corvette with the top down.
They like being seen in public
with a wealthy trophy hunter.

      Red knows how far a little flash
      can get someone like him.

His success is mythic to those
he allows to bask in his shadow,
submit themselves to his branding,
follow in his entourage.

Red is the prince of the neo
counterculture, the messiah
of transaction come now to bless
the worthy, share his rarified air.

      He knows his value. He's bought
      it all with other peoples' sweat.

Red walks into a bar and
a party breaks out, loud brazen
adoration until every bottle
is empty and shattered on the floor.

Then he slinks out a secret door,
leaves his acolytes drained, fearful,
envious of his excesses,
accountable for his bar tab.

Yes, everyone loves Red, but
not as much as he loves himself.

Darkness

I love the sound of breaking glass
as much as the next man, the crash
of flame-charged shards on concrete

grinding under booted feet,
the stinging smell of teargas like
cloudy sails carried by the wind.

I love how fire warms your cheeks,
burns passion into passive eyes, licks
a dark sky with its many tongues.

The space between us, you and I,
is arm's length on Adirondack chairs,
a glass of wine in each of our hands.

In the space beyond the reach
of our quiet fire, people hurl
themselves at history, ignite

a darkness they know better
than us, a darkness that singes
their souls every day, every night.

I would reach into their darkness
and say there is a place for them here
by our fire, but they won't hear me.

They are consumed by the sound of
their own voices finally being heard.
We sit at our silent pit and listen.

Diluting Red

How do you dilute a primary color
when no other primary will do?

You could add white, but
isn't white part of the problem?
Isn't white already implied,
a silent, preferred attribute for
any equal partnership with Red?

Options are like *compromise*:
a dirty word, a blurring of identity.
And let's be honest: diversity
is not this color's strongest suit.

Red is uneasy around contrasting colors,
suspicious of unfamiliar shades,
rejects watered-down versions
of its own distinctiveness.

But what is left?

Consider the range of blended alternatives:
orange to purple to muddy brown, it's hard
to imagine a partner more appropriate
for Red than white.

The result would be a hue to maintain
purity of heritage (in smaller doses),
with only the stigma of marching
into battle at the Capitol and
beyond, wielding a pink rally flag.

Fathers' Day

At 8 a.m. in Jonesville, Virginia
on a sunny Sunday morning even
the churches aren't open for business.
I roll up to a four-way, brake obediently,
proceed through the empty intersection
without touching my feet to the ground.

It's Father's Day and my father
is gone. My son is five hundred miles
away and probably still in bed. When
he finally wakes, his first concern will
be spending time with his own children.

I'm five hours from home, puttering
in low gear past houses butted up
against the berm, trying to not disturb
residents in this quiet town beside
a two-lane highway that winds from
Kentucky to Virginia to Tennessee.

It's Father's Day and I'm taking
a long ride alone through peaceful
places, thinking about my father and
how little I did for him on this, his day,
while he was alive. A card, a call,
maybe dinner if I was in town.

On a break ahead, I find a text
from my son before I slide
my phone back into a pocket,
feel it vibrate occasionally
as the sun climbs the sky
and bastes me in my own reverie.

I break beneath a tree at Lake Lure where
other riders are gathered, spot a father and son
on sport bikes stacked high with travel bags.
They're all geared-up in armor, full-face helmets
with mikes, but still discuss the road ahead:
which gear is best for which turn; who should lead.

Sounds like too much planning for my taste.

Down to a t-shirt now, my riding jacket
is bungied to my dry bag which is bungied
to the passenger seat. I remove my half-shell,
hair soaked in sweat, and wonder how
those guys ride in all that shit—but as they
roll away, I must confess: *They do look sporty.*

Forty miles down the road, I'll catch
and blow past them as we enter Shelby.

My son's text says he also plans to ride today.
He has a sport bike and slick gear, too.
I raise a two-finger salute to other riders I pass.
Some are fathers who chose to spend today
on two wheels as well and it occurs to me:

I rarely see their faces well enough
to recognize them if we ever meet again.
My own son could roll by in the opposite
direction and neither of us might know,
both focused on our own destinations, both
loaded down with our own form of baggage.

Forgiving Red

"For what?" it asks
in self-righteous indignation
as you stare into the many blank eyes
of obsessive faultlessness.

You can't dent this dogma
of exceptionalism. *Red is
as Red does* and this petulant
child can deftly disguise itself

in patriarchal entitlement, paint
itself with victimhood, wear
the fraudulent mask of persecution
as well as any doomed messiah.

Do you forgive a perpetrator
who shows no remorse? No shame?
A burglar who breaks into your house,
waves a gun in your wife's face,
then shrugs it off when apprehended?

You can forgive the lion for killing a gazelle—
it is its nature. The same for the lifeless gift
your tabby deposits on your back porch.

You can forgive a wrong number at 3am,
the ding on your car door in the grocery store
parking lot, pinot noir on a favorite white sweater,
dog shit on brand new carpet.

You plan for unplanned mishaps like these.
Murderous insurrection is something else.

Meanwhile, they huddle like a scrum
of naked Spartan wannabes, guard
each other's backsides as if the rest
of us can't already see their bare asses.

And you have to wonder:
Does Red see itself for what it has become?

Until it does, all you can do is rub
its nose in its own mess, smack its ass,
say, "bad boy," and let forgiveness
find its own justification.

Good Guys

I found them in the morning
under the Christmas tree, shiny
steel barrel, white plastic grips,
twin holsters on a leather belt,
an ample supply of rolled red caps.

I didn't see anything else,
tore the package open, tightened
the belt over my pajamas, strapped
the holsters to my legs with rawhide laces—
quick-draw style. Mother asked,
"What about your other gifts?"

I paused from gunning practice,
turned back to the tree. There among
the filler gifts: games and educational ploys,
hid a large gift-wrapped box
with my name on it. I shredded
wrapping paper and ripped open
the taped box to find a cowboy hat,
vest, and chaps   *all in red*.

Red has never been my color.

Even at six-years-old, I knew
it as the color of boastful people,
loud cars, flashy clothes, tomatoes,
and lipstick that made women's lips
scream for attention.

Cowboys don't wear red, I thought,
It's the color of dandies and city slickers.

My mother must have read my mind
and begged me to put them on for
the Christmas picture I confiscated
long ago and stashed in my attic.

I remember her coaxing me, saying
red was the color the good guys wear.
I didn't believe it then.
I believe it less now.

Harmony

A buyer asked about a missing order:
When did it ship? When would it arrive?
Could I provide a tracking number?

His address was in Harmony,
Pennsylvania, a place I knew well
from a single visit long ago.

> I wanted to tell him a story
> about a Sunday night in 1979.
> It featured a young couple,
> a crying baby, a '65 Ambassador
> with bald tires, a blown head gasket,
> and a Dairy Queen manager who
> insisted an order had to be placed
> before he'd lend us *his* phone.

Tracking said the package was
undeliverable as addressed and held
at the local Post Office for pick up.

I relayed this information
and tracking number to the buyer,
repressing an urge to say more.

> I wanted to tell him how I
> remember this tiny town
> beside I-79 with no
> northbound re-entry;
> how dark the highway;
> how cold the air; how dry
> a *Brazier Burger* tastes when
> bought with your last dollar.

It Is What It Is

Winding through
the countryside,
windows wide open,
she asks me if I smell it.
"What," I say, "the cow shit?"
She tells me it's not *cow shit*
but *horse shit* and I apologize
for not being the same
manure connoisseur
she thought she married.
Time changes everyone.
I've stepped around or over
each load of crap someone else
dropped in my path, risen above
the messes others have dumped
on me, shoveled my share of stink,
and one thing I know:
        Shit is shit.
You can shame it, rename it,
blame it on someone else,
cover it up with dirt or cologne,
but when you leave it
for someone else to clean up,
smell is not the issue.

II

Living in a Red State Blues, Part 2

People are crazy and times are strange
I'm locked in tight, I'm out of range
I used to care, but things have changed
　　　　~Bob Dylan from "Things Have Changed"

My chapped lips kiss the wind
while they mouth the words
to a ballad that's been camped out
in my head for the last hundred miles,
a gravelly voice grinding down
the pretext that *we are all*
in this together, that we are all
brothers on the road. After a pitstop
at a gas-n-go in *Nowhereville*,
it was easy to see the drawn lines
drifting apart, frayed threads of
a flag shredding in the wind.
Other bikers, dayworkers, a family
on the way to or from church,
strangers sharing friendly nods,
a wave, warm regards—all fade
to wariness when they see me
pull a mask from my pocket,
hang it from my ears to cover
my nose and mouth as I walk
to the door. I am now *other*,
an enemy in this state
of mind where anyone who
doesn't echo dominant pre-
conceptions and mis-
conceptions can't be trusted;
can't be one of *US*.
The bard's words keep rolling
to the hum of my tires on asphalt,
hypocrisy becoming clearer

with each two-finger salute
to a passing biker who is hidden
behind a helmet or dark glasses
and neck gaiter.
We're all so full of shit.
The church guy in his black Lexus
keeps a MAGA hat in the back seat
for special occasions. His wife wears
her flowery polyester dresses prim
and proper for an hour on Sundays,
is bound tight to him and this way
of life, but keeps a little black skirt
in the closet because you never know
when a tempest might come
and blow it all away.

March 13

Today is the anniversary of my
father's death, or was it the day before
when his eyes last opened or the week before
when he froze in mid-sentence, rigid fingers
reaching up to still air for stray words
that never returned to him again.

His words find me at odd times.

> *It's only the last two minutes*
> *of the game that matter*

But it's unspoken moments
that haunt me most, moments
that echo throughout my day: the way
he turned a cereal spoon upside down
on the table when he was finished eating,
peanut butter spread to the edge
of a Ritz, a dab of Smucker's
black raspberry jelly in the middle.

> *knowledge is the only thing that's truly yours,*
> *the only thing they can never take away.*

On a shelf above my head he sits,
an eight-year-old on a black and white pony,
tall and proud, fists full of reigns. Sometimes
I look up to that pony boy and chuckle knowing
his parents paid a nickel to have it taken at
a carnival, how it was the closest he ever got
to riding a real horse, city boy that he was.

> *if you're going to do something,*
> *don't do it half-assed*

I thought of my father every day
of the week leading up to this date,
but morning found me immersed in work,
the work he taught me, a job he envied.
When my nephew texted a photo of
his grandfather in a 1940s Navy uniform,
shame swept a chill through me, realizing
I'd almost let the day slip by neglected.

*do unto others as you would have them
do unto you*

I look up at the pony boy on the shelf
and remember why, of all the photos
I have of him, I choose to display this one.
It's because it frames him as someone
I know he never was, but reminds me
of his most cherished gift to me:
a sense of wonder, imagination,
the foresight to perceive the possible.

*face the music, even when
you don't like the tune*

I am my father's dreamer son,
the one who sometimes loses track
of time, the one who's been tossed
from numerous horses, landed hard,
but always found a nickel to climb back on
because that's what he expects of me.
While I may forget days and dates,
I will never forget that. Not that.

Neoconservatives

It's like bursting in
on grandma and grandpa
doing the nasty, two
octogenarians wriggling
against each other on
the living room sofa,
clothes, glasses, and canes
strewn to places their hands
can't reach when the action
is over.

You stand transfixed
by the moment,
the awkwardness of it all,
arthritic fingers flapping
for handholds on wrinkled flesh,
grandma's eyes glazed open
like prey in a leopard's jaws.

Worst of all, you know
they know you are there,
they know you are watching,
they know that no amount
of pleasure they feel will ever
heal your scorched eyes
or make that couch
look comfortable again.

Punishing Red

You know a smack across
the knuckles won't be enough,
won't stem a pattern of misbehavior
and harsher measures will only
escalate to never ending retribution.

You've seen this before.
The resistance to any form
of discipline, any concession that
the color of the world could be
different from the color of one's heart.

You know the climax
of corporal punishment
is often bloody. You sit Red
in a corner by itself, leave it
to consider the error of its ways.

Soon you realize your mistake,
watch it stare where two walls meet.
Red doesn't see a joining or blending.
It sees a bent and folded reality,
a single wall wedged into itself.

You try to turn him around, open
him up to face the room, but Red
likes these confines, sees the room's
broad expanse as another oppressive
threat to his sense of exceptionalism.

Red Roads

The winter solstice of 2020,
crisp and clean, with a sky so blue
it shouts: "Get out! Get out!"

So we do. At the tail end
of a claustrophobic year
of sordid unprecedence

we escape restraints and ride
the red roads of divided America
embellished in denial.

On the shortest day of
the longest year we see signs
of disunity everywhere.

Unwilling to concede the end
is near, they stand firm, defiant,
reliably rigid against reality.

Scattered flags of the same
phylum, hang limp and lonely,
awaiting the afterlife of a relic,
a souvenir of a time gone by.

Redbirds

We were Redbirds once. Twice
a week we'd carpool from our homes
in Warwood, proudly wear our red caps
with the bold white Rs onto the field
on Wheeling Island.
They've built a racetrack and casino where
the field once stood, a football stadium
across the many parking lots—
something we sorely needed back then.
To a twelve-year-old, those bright red hats
were a badge of honor in a small town
that could only afford to support one team.
We wore them everywhere.
Our neighbors knew us, knew we
were winners, hard-nosed, reliable, never
surrender until the last out is called.
We were Redbirds.
I thought about my Redbird days
as I watched men in red hats
storm the Capitol Building,
beat police with flags, sticks, bats;
spray them with bear repellent
and wondered about the symbolism.
Would a young player today,
whose team colors and hat were red,
wear that hat around town with
the same amount of pride we did,
or fold it into a glove, then chuck it
deep into a corner of a closet after
the game or season was over?

Rehabilitating Red

For years it's been stacked
on the shoulders of others,
white and blue let it have
top billing, a lead role
in a revered ensemble.

Maybe that was the mistake.
Maybe rotating the order
in which credits were given
would have stymied the diva
that dwelled within.

It's a hard fall from there
to understudy, an alternate
among the peers it once
considered less worthy
than itself.

Resurrecting a career will
be hard for a color so proud
of its purity, its independence
from the artlessness of
the rest of the cast.

We can suggest the usual
cliches: *bootstraps, new beginnings,*
but until Red concedes it needs
an intervention, it will remain
a glittery wannabe
in a chorus line of many.

Reunion in an Airport Restroom

What do you do when
the man at the adjacent urinal
starts a conversation as if
resuming a thought left hanging
with a long-lost relative at
a wedding or picnic. You,
having held silent the business
at hand, the business for which
you have waited for hours stuffed
into a flying steel barrel, your
plumbing aching to be drained
for so long now that, amid this
scintillating discussion, it
sputters to a slow rebellious
drip, but wait, did he ask
a question; try to divert you
from your primary purpose
in this porcelain concourse,
where all the gates are full
and a line runs from the door
to the tarmac; try to draw you
out of your self-conscious state,
shake off antisocial incivility,
embrace your fellow man?

The Color of Fraud

We live messy lives out here,
past where the sidewalks end
and roads narrow so much a tractor
can barely pull a combine between
the ditches on either side.

A place where old barns melt
into mud and take Grandad's
dead Studebaker with them;
where cow shit yields corn rows,
billy goats trim lawns, and what they
won't eat the earth eventually swallows.

Rusty machinery parts and broken toys
lean against the weathered wood
of a porch, itself a depository
for worn furniture and museum pieces.

Out back a white International box truck
rests on cracked tires, spills laundry
from torn cartons on its liftgate like
tissue hanging from the heel of a shoe.

In this land of green and gold and brown,
Red is a superstar, a celebrity spotlighting
a glorious past, *stolen*, but still within reach
if not for… because of… an ideology of blame,
of *whatifism* and *whataboutism*,

a dazzling ornament spinning
cotton candy promises at a carnival
for cancel cultural cultists, masking
reality as if slapping a coat of paint
on it could fix the underlying rot.

The New South

A midday moon ghosts
the cloudless blue over
my shoulder, above
a winding country road
that outlines pastures pocked
with patches of young growth
and swabs of cotton stubbornly
clinging to field stubble,
remnants of last year's harvest.

I know every curve of this
route intimately like a long-
time lover, its tender spots,
its dark corners where
Confederate flags still fly.
Each time I pass one, I want
to light it up, torch it, watch
each thread burn, lose color
and curl into dust like the nation
and sentiment it represents.

But that would be politically
incorrect here, where so many
hide everything in the open
under a banner of *heritage*.
They say, "It's none of your business,"
as if none of my people fought
or died in that same war; say,
"You're not from around here.
You don't understand."

Oh, but I do; I really do.

Twenty Years Later

I remember a school
of silver sky fish shimmering
against a clear blue backdrop.

My first thought was: This is how
vultures circle over a wounded animal,
waiting for the inevitable.

But they didn't glide as if at home.
They cut and banked more like frantic
sharks when blood is in the water.

Blood was in the air that day.
Even before I knew, I knew
something was wrong.

My highway ride to morning class
was trafficless for once. The only sound
was tire rubber humming on asphalt.

Parking spaces were plentiful and
I wondered if I'd missed a memo:
"Take the day off; go for a ride."

When a student parked nearby
I asked, "What's with all the planes?"
and she told me.

Glancing back to that moment
and every moment since we huddled
around a small teachers' lounge tv,

watched a second plane spear
the second tower, knowing we
were under attack, knowing planes

swarmed overhead as someone sorted
friend from foe, I wonder now if we
will ever know the difference again.

Assessing the VRBO

It was the best mountain view we'd seen
since we started guesting in these
lazy hills where locals proudly plod
along on *mountain time,* a pace
akin to a California surf shop.

The listing said, *Perfect for two couples —*
but I suspect that only severely close friends
or a family with young children, could
lodge themselves in this cottage
without leaving as enemies.

The house was clean, appliances worked,
a mishmash of Americana warmed
the front room that overlooked
a small yard spilling down to the street
with public parking on the other side.

At 6am, a heavy androgynous person
started cutting adjacent lawns.
All of them. By my count, two
passes each at perpendicular angles,
finally finishing by early afternoon.

I tried to imagine the original
owners raising a family in such
a compact space: two bedrooms, one bath
with shower, living room, dining room, kitchen
shoehorned into one thousand square feet,

planted on a tenth of an acre of hillside,
beside the Church of Christ, catty-corner
from City Park, the town cemetery across
the street with a parking lot wedged neatly
between home and eternal rest.

Cradle to grave in one small-town block
where everyone gathers sometime: joggers,
dog walkers, lovers, parents with children.
Here resides a slice of pie out of time,
a cloistered community comfort zone.

I see it now in summers gone by,
people seated on the front stoop
or lawn chairs, watching basketball,
tennis, youth baseball; a faint scent
of fried chicken wafting through the air.

An American Rant

I never say fuck in a poem, but I'm speaking for the
soul of America and America's soul is dying, it's
fucking dying, and that's the second time I've said fuck
in this poem, and it's important because the folks who
are killing America need to hear it in a way that opens
their fucking eyes to something other than their own
fragmented piece of a shrinking pie, slicing itself up,
sliding down the drain like ice cream or whip cream
and I scream for the deserted solitary silent moments
we each keep locked up inside our personal prisons,
clawing at our inner walls, hoping to shred the divided
states of America's imperfect disunity of socio-
economic-racial-class-defining bullshit that's built so
one guy in a black Lexus—black because this is where
black really matters—can keep a firm grip on the top
rung and grant everyone beneath him the freedom to
live in his shadow. Or not. As if all he can think about
is: *It's Thanksgiving, the hot water heater has died, and the
plumber can't make it because he's spending one of three
days he takes off each year with his own family and how dare
he when company is coming at 2 and the kickoff is at 4.* He
wants us all high, inebriated, numb to the dumbness
that feeds his wealth, but someone's got to take out the
trash, someone has to man the Seven Eleven 24/7 for
his convenience because that must be our top priority,
even on the holiest of days. He preaches capitalism, rigs
the marketplace, dictates the value of other peoples'
lives, blankets himself with a bible he misinterprets to
best suit his needs of the moment and he's too dense
to see the subtle irony, the blatant fucking hypocrisy.
Or is he?

Consoling Red
(AKA: *Hugging a Snake*)

You want to put your arm around him,
say "There, there; everything will be fine,"
but you know you can't sell anyone
anything you wouldn't buy yourself, and
this character has been known to slither
out from under other obligations.

Red says, *Blue always squeals on me*
and Black takes without asking permission.
"Would you rather be Black or Blue?" you ask,
hearing his answer retch from deep within.
His pain is a product of fear, envy, lies,
weaponized by his own vindictiveness.

He's a child who has everything,
who believes he's entitled to the best
of everything; a child who doesn't play nice
with anyone, who builds roadblocks
to prosperity, walls to keep others
away from the good stuff, *his* good stuff.

Red's unscarred voice proclaims:
        You must bleed first to earn a place here.
        You must sacrifice your children.
This is what he calls winning.

He doesn't believe in consolation prizes.
Winning isn't everything, winning is the only thing.
He's all in all the time, tilts the table, loads
the dice, takes preventative measures
against any other outcome.

You enter his world knowing
the rules are rigged against you.
When you persist, you find him
waiting in the middle of your path,
rattle chattering desperately.

You try to negotiate around him.
That's when he strikes. That's why
he strikes; and you learn a valuable lesson:
You can't bargain with a snake, can't
please a snake, can't comfort a snake.
It is a snake. It will always be a snake.
That's all you can expect from a snake.

Legacy

1.

My mother's father was broad
and rigid as an Appalachian mountain.
Fists clenched tight as boulders,
he stood his ground, defiant
in the face of casual interactions.

He planted himself at the foot
of the table, scowled at his wife
at the other end who avoided
eye contact as she muttered
her disdain for him.

Happiness was not his virtue; joy
a foreign concept. A welder by trade,
he brought home metal scraps, shaped them
into tools to frustrate his internment:
knives, spears, rifles, cannons.

He considered himself a gunsmith,
rebuilding, reboring, reloading casings
he collected at gun ranges. I still see him
sunken deep into the cushions of a broken
recliner he could barely climb out of,

a juice glass full of bourbon on
a table beside him, a beanbag ashtray
keeping it company, overflowing
with the snuffed-out remnants
of hand-rolled cigarettes.

2.

My father's father was
the Monongahela River in winter:
a placid, unbroken surface, hiding
an effortless undercurrent.

He never raised his voice, not even
to say hello from across Penn Avenue.
He'd come to you, listen to you, speak
softly, seldom, but when he did,
it was always worth hearing.

The son of an alcoholic with
eleven siblings, he traded school
for a job during the Great Depression
to help put food on the family table.

An avid gardener, a Mason,
a handyman who understood
the workings of tools and people,
he spent the last 25 years of his life
caring for a fragile wife.

A card shark at Bridge and Pinochle,
he'd sometimes sip wine and tug gently on
a *Tiparillo* (if he wasn't chewing *Elephant Butts*).
He acted as if he was studying the game,
when he was really studying you.

3.

My father liked to laugh, liked life
uncomplicated, believed in loyalty,
honesty, hard work. He was never
a boy scout, but they may as well
have used him as a poster boy.

He was a meat and potato guy:
took care of his family and made no
demands on the rest of the world, kept
his sense of humor, his dignity even when
the world dumped its trash on him.

Twice he came to get me from the arms
of the law in the wee hours of the morning.
He even convinced my mother once that
a hangover was the best punishment
for a first-time drunk.

It wasn't until he died that the rest
of the world learned our secret,
that I was his adopted son, someone
else's mistake that he stood up for,
gave a name, a home, principles.

4.

I am not my father, but I am
my father's son, the creation
he shaped from inherited clay;
his voice the conscience against
which everything is measured.

But I can't see the world through
his eyes, enter each day with the same
unswaying optimism, the same
conviction that he could handle
whatever shit the world served up.

I am not my father, not a barge
my mother's father welded together,
adrift on my other grandfather's subtle currents.
I am a boulder in the rapids, a tugboat
pushing a heavy load upstream.

If I believed in prayer, I would pray
that my son and his son and all the sons
and daughters yet to come, remember
we are more than the blood in our veins
we are a river, a rock, the current.

Anachronism

My father checked out at the right time.
He would have hated living now,
in this era where truth is a bitcoin
with no anchor, no measurable value.

He was an Eisenhower Republican,
a sailor at the end of the last great war,
a student of history until his vision
hindered his ability to read.

No more papers or magazines, but he
could smell the festering load of elephant dung
before the red wave arrived, metastasized,
permeated the air with a haze of corruption.

I see him now in my youngest brother,
escaping to the safety of sixties sitcoms,
the white noise of laugh tracks whispering
in the background of work-from-home days.

Some people find comfort in the past, I guess,
comfort also in a quick exit stage left
when the right has been obstructed, lost
in a cloud of *Outer Limits* screen snow.

A Tinderbox of Unsubtle Discourse

It is the law: as a civilization dies and goes down
to eat ashes along with all other dead civilizations
—it is the law all dirty wild dreamers die first—
gag 'em, lock 'em up, get 'em bumped off.

And since at the gates of tombs silence is a gift,
Be silent about it, yes, be silent—forget it.

~Carl Sandburg from "At the Gates of Tombs"

There are those who prefer silence
to the sound of the wind in the trees.
For them, my voice rustles their peace
like a harsh, unwelcome breeze.

I am the ghost of a storm they
would rather forget, as if they
believe a wave of their hand could
disperse an approaching hurricane.

There's a red sky this morning,
red as the hot California hills,
and they think they can wish it
away with happy thoughts.

The wind has had its day, they say.
They want to muffle it, muzzle
the barking dog that wakes them,
shakes them from their comfort zone.

I am an inconvenient dog,
a crusty leaf skittering down the road,
a spark dropped in a dry forest:
Pretending won't make me go away.

Special Thanks

I'm too bossy to belong to most writing groups, but I have friends who are poets and don't mind offering feedback. When I need an ego boost, I always go to my good friend, Jonathan K. Rice. He will catch my changes in tense and perspective and spelling, but critiquing… Jonathan likes everything. There is not a more eclectic and optimistic human being on the planet. People like him make you feel good about what you are doing and push through your doubts.

I'd also like to thank others who have contributed to shaping this collection: Rick Campbell, Keith Flynn, Anne Kaylor, James Kaylor, Denton Loving, Leslie Ann Mcilroy, Richard Peabody, Pat Riviere-Seel, Maria Rouphail, Richard Allen Taylor, Steve Taylor, Barrett Warner, Jesse Waters.